D1496250

Bowl (author's work).

Tetrahedral honey pot with hand-carved dipper (author's work).

Making
Native American
Pottery

by Michael W. Simpson

Naturegraph Publishers, Inc.

Library of Congress Cataloging-in-Publication Data
Simpson, Michael W.
　Making native American pottery　/　by Michael W.
Simpson.

　　1.　Catawba Indians—Pottery.　2. Pottery craft—South
Carolina. I　Title.
E99.C24S56 1991　　　　　　　　　　　　　　　　90-5836
738.1'4—dc20　　　　　　　　　　　　　　　　　　　CIP

　ISBN 10:　0-87961-191-X
　ISBN 13:　978-0-87961-191-0

2019 Printing

Naturegraph Publishers has been publishing books on
natural history, Native Americans, and outdoor subjects
since 1946. Free catalog available

Books for a better world

Naturegraph Publishers, Inc.
PO Box 1047 • 3543 Indian Creek Rd.
Happy Camp, CA 96039
(530) 493-5353
www.naturegraph.com

In memory of Doris Blue.

Fired pots, cleaned and rubbed with a soft cloth (author's work).

Fired pots (author's work).

Fired pots (author's work).

Creamer and sugar bowl set by the author. Note the
rich variation in color; black, white, red, etc.

Special thanks to
Jayne Henderson

Table of Contents

Doris Blue holding a wedding vase she made.

The Story of Doris Blue

Doris Blue is the last living full-blooded Catawba Indian. She lives (since this writing she's died—1986) with her daughter on the Catawba Indian Reservation outside of Rock Hill, South Carolina, among the rolling hills that have been the home of her people for untold centuries.

My meeting with Doris was almost an accident. I was speaking with my wife-to-be one warm afternoon. Summer was nearing, and she was almost finished with her college art studies. "What would you like to do with your life after school is over?" I asked her. "I'd like to make pottery and fire it in the back yard, sell it to others, and maybe teach." She looked over the back yard doubtfully. I put my arm around her shoulders, "O.K. I'll see what can be done."

I had seen some unusual pottery for sale at a vegetarian restaurant. The multi-colored figurines, pipe bowls, and small dishes looked handmade. They were fired by a method unknown to me. Inquiring around, I finally met a man who owned one of the pipe bowls. He told me he didn't buy it at the restaurant, but at the home of an old Indian lady who made lots of pottery and fired it in her back yard. Persuading him to give me her address, I found her phone number and called to set up an interview and photo session. About a month after my fiancée had discussed her future hopes with me, I arrived at the door of Doris Blue, and there I also discovered a piece of my own past.

I am part Cherokee, a tribe indigenous to the Smokey and Blue Ridge Mountain Region, and next-door-neighbors, so to speak, with the Catawba. In fact, historically speaking, the two tribes were bitter enemies, constantly engaging in border fights over hunting territory and traveling rights.

I was, at the time, researching my geneology, and these parts of history were quite interesting. Doris elaborated upon a time when few records were kept.

Back in the 1800's native peoples were being "terminated" and displaced at an ever increasing rate. The Catawba were not a very large group, and so were no more immune to the plague of termination than they had been to smallpox and alcohol in the previous century.

When the Catawba were terminated they went up to live with their previous enemies in the mountains of North Carolina. They now were bound together in the struggle to remain in their homelands and preserve their cultures. The Catawba and Cherokee pottery families intermarried. A cross-fertilization of methods took place, with the final result being that the Cherokee adopted the Catawba method of firing pottery in an open pit, abandoning forever the traditional mound firing method, which has been nearly forgotten in modern times.

After some years passed the Catawba were reinstated and given federal recognition and their lands—much reduced of course—to return to. There they carried on with their way of life, incorporating new ways as needed, preserving the old ways as best they could.

The Cherokee were then, as had happened since the arrival of the first Europeans, forever changed. As with most tribes, copper, porcelain, silver, tin, and glass quickly replaced clay pottery in most practical uses due to their superior strength and durability. With cultural dispersion, and the influence of the Catawba people and methods, the old ways of the Cherokee became retired to vague references in dusty, outdated texts, written when indigenous peoples were still considered sub-human barbarians or inferior racial novelties.

Doris told me stories that taught me how to look to the earth for clay, to gather and purify it for use, and to use the old methods to build traditional pots. She also showed me how to fire pottery in my back yard without a kiln. For all her ancient wisdom I am thankful, and to her grandmothers, and her daughter who have handed down and preserved this prehistoric knowledge.

Doris taught me of the types of clay, the forms and designs common to her tribe's tradition, the woods I would need, the methods, and the hints gleaned from many generations of potters. She felt it sad that her own people are losing their traditions, that the young show little interest in traditional ways, and that the world is not as balanced as it was in past times. But she still has, at 82 years of age, the indomitable spirit of her people and the pride that is deservedly theirs for surviving into modern times, preserving their heritage and passing it on to those, such as myself, who wish to share the old ways with others.

For seven years I taught the lessons Doris gave me to thousands of young people in the schools of southwestern Oregon, which is my home. I am also part Yakima, born in Oregon. Now I wish to share the lessons of a grandmother with others, in the form of this book.

Doris has seen her work exhibited in galleries throughout the South, and sold her pottery to people across the country. A film has been made of her work, and she has exhibited her work and methods at the Smithsonian Institute. Although she has retired from making pottery, her daughter carries on the traditions, along with a few others such as myself, who have learned from them.

What you find in this book began with and originally came from Doris, although I have added considerably to my knowledge through practice over the years, and through study of the methods of many tribes. I have set down here a comprehensive overview of these varied methods of making and firing pottery used all across the North American continent, and will use examples from the Catawba, Cherokee, Hopi, Pueblo, and other tribes to enrich and augment what Doris gave me. I herein share my learning by expressing the traditional way fused with modern methods, materials, and means. I have expanded upon or altered the old ways only to update and simplify them, and to make them relevant and useful to all people.

Following is a short interview with Doris, wherein she speaks to everyone in her profound and quiet way of the traditions that are at the root of her ancient strength, and of the meaning of pre-technological society and its changing ways.

For my part, I will close by saying that my wife indeed obtained her wish, and that I found my way into a path I will follow all my life. I owe this to Doris, whom I thank profoundly. Now let her speak in her own words:

Doris, how did you become a potter?
My mother taught me, and my grandmother taught her.
How old is the Catawba method of making and firing pottery?
Nobody knows. It's been handed down for as long as anyone remembers.
How do you get your clay?
I take a shovel and bucket and go to a place not far from my house, here on the reservation, and dig it up. I bring it home, clean it through a screen, and store it.
Would anyone be able to find clay where you do?
Clay can be found anywhere, if you know what to look for. Only tribal members are allowed to dig clay here. Catawba potters have been digging clay in this place for a long time.
How long does it take to make and fire a pot?
From several days to many weeks depending on the type and size.

How do you make your pottery?

By hand. I use a few things, like shaping and burnishing stones, and sometimes wooden molds. But I work with the piece of pottery on my lap, or on the table. With a molded pot I form it, hollow it out, burnish, and dry it.

Could you tell me a little more about burnishing?

It's a way of rubbing the pottery with a piece of stone or bone to make it smooth—some of my burnishing stones were analyzed and found to be mastadon teeth!

Are the old ways of making and firing pottery being passed on to the next generation?

No.

Why not?

Because they aren't interested. Besides my daughter, almost no one has learned what I know.

How do you fire your pottery?

Outdoors, in a shallow firing pit. I preheat them in the oven, but that used to be done around the fire. Oak and maple are used to make a pile of coals. The pottery is arranged on the coals, and then covered with branches of pine to burn hot for a few more hours.

What makes the unique colors on the pottery?

The fire. You can't control it. Sometimes things come out really nice, sometimes they don't.

Are the pots waterproof?

No.

Could you say something about traditional forms?

I make smoking pipe bowls, water jars, storage containers, and bowls. Most forms had a particular use before clay was pushed aside by copper and silver for most uses.

Of the various methods of making North American pottery, the Catawba way is relatively simple, but do you have any tips for those who might choose to try it?

Be careful. Take your time. Life's moving too fast now.

Beginning With The Earth

Clay is the most durable of human creations when formed and fired. Other than stone, the earliest remains of civilized people are made of fire-hardened clay objects. Even the earliest writings given to our time were initially recorded on clay tablets.

Clay can be found almost anywhere. It hides beneath the topsoil and is sometimes unearthed during construction or road working projects. Traditionally clay was found along waterways, or in low, wet areas. Ancestral clay pits, whose secret locations are revealed only to apprentice potters, are the prized digs of many North American tribes.

Usually, upturned earth exists in layers. Topsoil is first, with sand and clay mixed together next. When this second layer is dried solid, it is often referred to as hardpan. Underneath the top two or three layers of soil, anywhere from a few inches to several feet down, you will often find usable clay that is clean and pure.

Pure clay is gray, being composed of aluminum and silicon. When these two minerals are hydrated, or "dripped" together in a solution, they combine and later solidify as the form of earth we call clay.

Pure clay is less common than mixed clay. A wide variety of other minerals are often present in a clay deposit, especially in sites that have been disturbed over geologic time. Erosion, earthquakes, and landslides are natural processes that both reveal and mix pure clay. You will often see red, yellow, or black color which indicates the presence of iron and its oxides.

Excavated site with chunks of dry clay to which the author is pointing.

A hillside next to a stream where clay might be found.

Bluish and purplish tints indicate the presence of manganese. White clay is mostly calcium and carbonate. Greenish, highly sticky clay has bentonite in it. Other shades and color mixes likewise show traces of a wide variety of mineral elements.

Clay is found in natural abundance and diversity the world over. All you need to do is seek it out, test it, and dig it up to take home and process for use.

The traditional clay of the Catawba is a beautiful yellow ochre. Cherokee people use red, brown, and grey clay—their nation covered five states and had many clay sites. Some Pueblo clays are full of mica chips that sparkle. Clays in the coastal Northwest are often pale blue. Iron pyrite flakes, high

Clay bed next to a stream.

silica sand, and other such substances give the clay objects of each tribe and region a unique feel and look that reflects the character and nature of the artists and their tribes.

Along streams, rivers, lakes, and even roadside ditches, and worksites where heavy, earthmoving equipment is used, as well as in your own back yard—are likely places to find this basic building material that has been used in the making of North American pottery for at least a few thousand years.

As an example of the widespread use and dispersion of clay objects through trade, I can cite the find of a friend of mine, in a field in the foothills of South Carolina, of a pipe bowl of Mayan origin! This might possibly lend support to some legends which say the Cherokee and Mayans were connected for centuries before the arrival of Europeans.

Pure clay, as the ancient craftmasters found, is a good find, but it cannot be shaped and fired in this state. It shrinks too fast during drying, and cracks. Mixed clays are better.

Truly usable clay has fine particles of sand or oxidized minerals in it. These particles aid in insuring slow, even shrinkage and drying of the piece both while it is being made and during the firing. Good mixed clays will dry properly, giving you ample time to work them, and they will hold their shape and not crack when subjected to the stresses of firing.

If the clay you find lacks this "grog," simply add some fine sand or ground up, already fired pottery. Put in just enough to make the clay slightly gritty and keep it from sticking to your hands. Even ashes from the fire pit can be used—some enterprising artisans even mix volcanic ash with their clays. Some experimenting will probably be needed to find the consistency and color you seek for your clay. And never be afraid to experiment—after all, it's only mud on the one hand, and our Mother Earth on the other.

As a general rule, the larger the pots you intend to build, the more grog you will need, up to a point. Smaller pieces can sometimes even be made of pure clay, if great care is taken to work fast and make near perfect curves the main shape.

You might find a good deposit of clay, but find it to be full of small roots, rocks, sticks, leaves, and other debris, which must, of course, be removed. Such materials, if not removed, will cause cracking or other flaws in finished pieces—if they don't explode in the fire!

In this case the clay must be processed before use. You can clean the wet clay by hand, if it's not too full of litter, by pressing it between your fingers and removing any debris you feel; or you can let it dry, break it down to a powder, then screen it to remove the excess pebbles, roots, and the like. Once you have a clean, dry powder you can remix with water and/or grog and minerals whenever you wish. Many older potters reform the powder into buns, or loaves, then dry these and store for later use.

When this process is completed you have a batch of clean, raw clay (not the same as pure clay) which is then ready to work into a smooth, wet ball to be used immediately or stored in a closed container.

If you prefer not to deal with processing clay, there are a number of fine commercially prepared clays that can be bought at artist's outlets, brickyards, or from those who collect it. Commercial clays come either wet or dry. You can get just about any color and mineral combination you want. Plus, these clays are already grogged and need little preparation. Just be sure that it is of the low-fire variety—any clay that will harden properly at less than 1500 degrees F. is fine. Consult with your supplier to obtain the proper clay.

Back to raw clay—what you'll have whether you make a ball of commercial clay or natural clay. It is best to let your raw clay cure for several days after it is prepared to be worked. This will insure even dispersal of moisture into all elements present. (Rainwater is the best mixer due to its "softness.") After your raw clay is cured it can be worked.

An alternative to the already described methods of

Some necessary tools; shovels, bucket, water . . . note the clay; dry to the left, curing in the bucket, processed to the right, stored in a plastic bag.

processing clay is that of sedimentation. In this method you mimic the natural process whereby clay is produced, although it does take more time. If you happen to gather a lot of clay at once though, this is the ideal method of dealing with cleaning and storage.

You can put your unprocessed clay in any large container—such as a plastic bucket—that won't rust and contaminate the clay with the colors of the material it's made of. Leave the clay in the bucket for at least two or three months, out in the open where rain can wash it for you. After enough time and settling underwater, the earth separates into its individual elements.

When you place your bucket out, put a fine mesh screen over the top to keep out bugs and leaves and things. When you dig into the clay you will find it has settled into definite layers. Pour off the water and let the bucket sit a while.

As you dig into the clay you will find the top layer to be fine, pure clay, in a sort of slurry, or liquid mud, that is useful for "slipping," or painting the completed pots later. Skim this "slip" off the top of the clay and store it in a closed container. The next, and thickest, layer will be of perfectly mixed clay with more grog the deeper you go, until nearing the bottom third you will begin to run into debris. At the bottom of the bucket you will find rocks, sticks, and other large matter.

This clay at the bottom can be cleaned and processed just like freshly gathered clay and used later. You can test the layered clay for proper consistency between your fingers, or, as one old brickmaker did, against a front tooth!

Whatever clay you use must be immediately worked, or processed and stored as is appropriate. If stored, it can be kept indefinitely either as a dry powder, or in wet balls in a closed container. Clay that is ready to work will be slippery, but not overly sticky, slightly gritty, consistent throughout.

A simple walk in the woods, a curious look at big machines upending the ground, or even watching a neighbor rototill his back yard garden—all provide occasions to find usable deposits of clay.

Throughout the tribal states and nations of what is now called North America, the earth has been searched and used for unrecorded centuries by the First People, the people of clay.

Preparing The Ground

When you finally have a usable ball of raw, cured clay you will need to begin to work it. You have about ten minutes at a time, between additions of water, to work on the clay. To work on the clay you must squeeze all the air pockets out through wedging, that is forcibly dropping the lump of clay on a hard surface, cutting it into several pieces, reuniting them, and repeating the process until the lump is of uniform consistency.

The clay must be smooth, have no air bubbles or foreign materials in it, and be moist enough to work into a shape without cracking (too dry), or sticking to your fingers or the table (too wet). Once the clay is cured, wedged, and rolled into smooth balls it is ready for you to decide how to use it.

Among certain tribes clay objects were considered to be alive. Others saw the clay object as a test of the person making it—how it came through the test of firing indicated the strength of one's character. Some of the People looked on both clay and fire, as well as air and water, as sacred gifts to them from the Creator.

The Mother Earth is sacred as well as the Father Sky. To ancient peoples such things were to be given reverence and respect. Living in equilibrium with their surroundings was the highest goal. It is still important that we treat the living Earth with respect. Don't destroy habitat or trespass in the process of gathering or moving clay. In either case, you might get your clay but lose a part of nature to carelessness. The results can be injury or prosecution.

Approach the Earth with respect. Some elder potters still

sing to the ground, ask permission to carry it away and burn it, kindle sage and tobacco offerings, and give thanks to it for sustaining them and giving of itself so freely, asking nothing in return but care.

Prepare yourself and the ground, and you are ready to begin making pottery the old way. All you will need are a few simple tools.

You will need a bowl of water and a towel, a lap board or solid table to work on. A large working area is desirable. You will need your clay, tools, and slip (fine slurry of clay used to paint designs onto pots).

Grinding raw clay into powder to mix with water.

Powdered clay partly ready to mix with water. Note balls of raw clay on the board.

Balls of prepared clay; to the left you can still see air bubbles inside the ball sliced in half, whereas the ball on the right is free of air and ready to use.

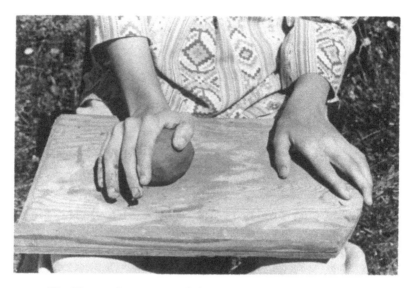

Rolling the second ball on the lap board.

Previous to working your clay, perhaps even while you are gathering materials, look for a variety of smooth stones of various shapes and sizes. These will be used to "burnish," or polish, the outer surface of the pottery later. Sharp stones can be used to apply designs and decorative markings, as can a sharp stick, or a wooden paddle. A small paint brush is used in applying slip, along with a fine brush to paint on designs.

A rag ring can be used to set the bottom of the pot in while you are working on it, as can a saucer. In any case you must use powdered clay or ashes on the bottom of the pot to keep it from sticking to things—or you can use the more modern material of a plastic baggie underneath the pot, or a paper towel.

To work on the wet pot as it shapes up you can use a piece of gourd, or a paddle and stone anvil. A piece of leather or a

Incising designs with a sharpened stick on the completed pot after it has dried just a little bit.

small brush can be used to smooth the pot as it nears completion.

Among the Catawba, and some other potters, wooden molds inherited from past generations, or carved new, are used to form pots. An old wooden or clay bowl or plate will do well as molds for beginners.

You will need a ventilated or very warm area to dry your clay pieces once they are done. And after they dry you will need sandpapper to striate the outer surface of the piece previous to application of slip and designs.

All of the items mentioned are readily available to most people at a minimum of time and expense.

With clay prepared, tools laid out, and work area ready, you can begin the processes of building pots with hand made, personally gathered materials and implements.

Building By Hand

You will need to work the ball of raw, mixed, cured, and wedged clay to perfect smoothness. All air pockets must be removed, and the outer surface must be smooth and free of both cracks and excessive moisture.

The ball of clay can be worked to perfect smoothness and even consistency by flattening it between your palms and rolling it back into a ball several times. It must be workable without cracking, while also not sticking to your fingers.

Clay is gathered in late spring and early summer, when the earth is damp, and neither too wet or too dry. It is worked and fired in summer, when the weather is warm and dry.

On any good day you can choose from several different ways to make traditional pottery. All of these begin with a ball of clay, an adequate work area, and a few tools.

The five most commonly used methods of making pottery among indigenous North Americans were: 1) the pinched pot, 2) the slab pot., 3) the coiled pot, 4) the molded pot, and 5) the hollow pot. The latter two methods are actually elaborations of the former three. A combination of two or three methods of working the clay were, and still are to this day, the general way. These basic methods are common the world over, but the North American peoples did some unique and exquisite works of art as they practiced their crafts.

More modern methods, such as the "wheel thrown" pot were not practiced in the Americas, although pots were sometimes, when very large, turned on a pedestal or movable platform. Thrown pots are too delicate and thin-walled to be

Rolling a ball of clay between the hands.

**Prepared ball of clay ready to work. Clay in hand
must still be rolled.**

fired in an open fire, but are excellent when fired in modern gas or electric kilns.

The stresses of open firing dictate that pots be thicker and curved in their construction. Thin walls and square corners .crack more readily. Properly made pots, constructed in the old way, will last a long time, as evidenced by ancient tribal sites throughout the continent.

It is easiest to start by making a pinched pot. With some experience you will be ready to make a slab pot, and then to learn the more intricate techniques of making a coiled pot. Last will be alternate methods such as molding pots and creating other complex forms, using the simple tools already described.

The Pinched Pot

Hold a prepared ball of clay in one hand—start small, with a ball 1" to 6" in diameter—and poke the thumb of your other hand into the center of the ball. Now you pinch the wall between your thumb and forefinger all the way around until it is of desired shape and thickness. Proper thickness is about one-half inch, or the thickness of your little finger, with the bottom of the pot and lowest portion of the wall being slightly thicker.

If you choose to work a larger ball, drop it onto a lap board or the table top (don't forget the ashes, powdered clay, or plastic bag to prevent sticking), then use the thumb and forefingers of both hands to pinch, form, and turn the pot.

Larger pinched pots are not encouraged unless they are made of commercial earthenware type clay. This is because the uneven pressures of pinching make the walls less stable than in slab and coil pots. Once you are more familiar with the methods and get a feel for working the clay it may then be possible to experiment with larger pinched pots. The pinching method is almost always best for forming the bases of larger pots that are to have slab or coiled walls. This will be covered later.

Balls of clay ready to work. Thumb is being pressed into the center of the ball of clay to open it up and make the rough form of a bowl to be pinched.

First step in a pinch pot; spreading the ball with thumbs.

Second step; pressing the sides of the bowl between thumbs and fingers.

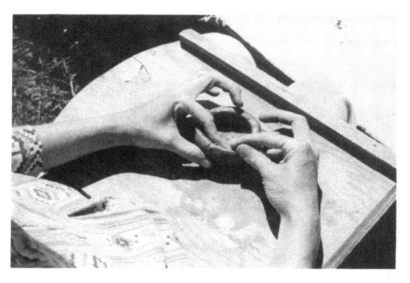

Third step; pinching the walls to proper thickness; moisture in clay is from dipping fingers in water as you go along.

Pinched bowl completed.

Make your pot round and sturdy, and in one piece until you are experienced with all the techniques. Streamlined or complex construction, and combined techniques can be dealt with later.

The Slab Pot

To make a slab pot flatten your ball of clay into a uniform pancake that is about ½" thick, or the thickness of your hand in the middle. This is your basic slab.

Use your thumbs and fingers to bend, shape, and pinch your slab into the desired form. Simple forms such as shallow bowls, small plates, medallions, and scallop-edged pots are best made using this method.

Another way to form a slab into a pot is to mold it over another bowl, saucer, or plate, using ashes, powdered clay, a plastic baggie, or even a very thin layer of vaseline between the clay and the object being used as a form.

Forming clay is the opposite of molding clay, where the clay is formed *inside* of a carved or poured mold. Molding is covered later.

Allow the slab to become semi-dry while still on the form. In this way the shape can "set." The outside can be smoothed, and even incised with decorations while still setting. When semi-dry it can be removed from the form and allowed to dry for later decoration.

Remove the slab pot from the form carefully to avoid cracking or altering its shape. Make sure to remove the clay object from the form before it dries all the way as a precaution against sticking and breakage. When the pot has set into its desired shape all you need to do is smooth the pot's lip with your fingers and a little water, then let it dry.

Pots must dry slowly and evenly. If they dry too quickly they will crack. They need at least 12 hours in a dry, warm climate. Where the climate is moist and/or cool it can take from 24 to 72 hours for the pots to become "leather hard," like rawhide. They must be stiff, but not totally dried if you wish to apply incised decoration; otherwise, they must be totally dry. You will know when a pot is dried completely because it will lighten up considerably in color and feel solid to the touch. Often it will have a hollow tone if tapped lightly.

When pots are finally dried, after 3 to 14 days, they are ready to be sanded, slipped, and otherwise decorated. Regardless of what method you use to build pots you will end up, at this point, with a dry, unfinished clay body ready for shaping and decoration.

Sometimes designs are incised very deeply and broadly into the surface of a semi-dry pot then filled with another color of clay upon drying. Design suggestions and methods will be covered later.

Some hints on shaping pots include: looking at the pot from all directions as you form it to insure that it's symmetrical, moistening your fingers every so often to prevent cracking while the pot is in formation, turning the pot as you work, making the walls of even thickness, making the lip even, and removing cracks with water and a little pressure. A plastic

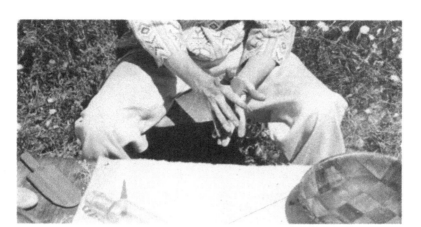

**First step in a slab pot; flattening the ball of clay
between palms of hands.**

spray bottle is useful for misting the pot as you work on it.

If the clay is too dry it will resist being formed and crack
as you work it. If it is too wet the walls will not hold their
shape. In either case it is best to return to the uniform ball and
start again.

A really great thing about clay is that it is a "plastic"
medium and can always be reformed, unlike stone and wood.
Also, the more uniform the clay and the walls made of it, the
better chances the pot has of making it through the fire.

A later development was that of the rolled slab. A stone
rolling pin was used to make a very uniform slab, evenly
pressed, and of greater strength as a result. Such a rolled slab is
especially good for making plates, saucers, and other flat
objects.

The rules of consistency, uniformity in thickness, and
curved form must be followed at all times in the making of
North American pottery, or it will most likely end up cracked
or broken.

As with the pinched pot and the coiled pot, the slab pot

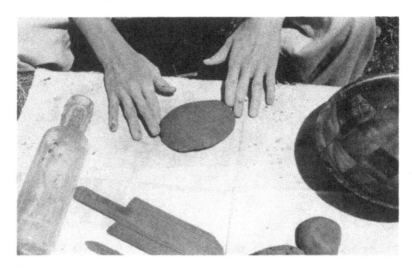

Slab ready to be rolled to even thickness. Note canvas covering on table, and some other useful tools such as a rolling pin, wooden paddle, sharpened stick, and bowl of water.

Rolling the slab to a uniform thickness.

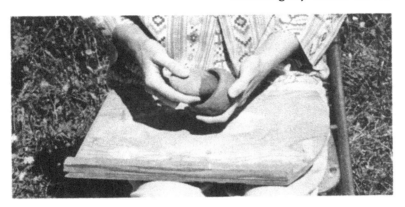

Continuing the shaping. Note that the stone has been dipped in water.

must have its outer and inner surfaces smoothed with moistened fingers when wet, and with tools later, when semi-dry or dried completely. The slab pot must also be pinched into final form in many cases. Likewise it must be allowed to dry slowly and completely, until such time as it is sanded, slipped, and decorated previous to firing.

The Coiled Pot

Just imagine what it would be like to have to make, by hand, from the ground up, once, twice, or even three times a year all the plates, cups, bowls, and cooking pots used in your home! That's just what native potters had to do. They learned that the pinch and slab pots are not as durable, and that they had to find better and easier ways to make pots last as long as possible. Out of necessity, pots were gradually constructed using methods and materials that had been continually refined over time; thus the coiled pot came into existence.

The coiled pot is stronger, can have thinner walls, and is more durable under repeated stress such as open cooking fires. Yet, other than the initial formation of the body of the clay object, the coiled pot is formed and finished in the same ways

Shaping a slab into a base for a coiled pot.

used with pinched and slab pots.

The first step in making a coiled pot is to form a base. You can form the base by either the pinch or slab method. The bottom will be flattened, and the sides, about an inch or two in height, will be the thickest parts of the walls to be built upon.

It is also easy to use the forming method to make a base, an old bowl begins a good shape. In any case, the base will be 1/2 to 2/3 the final width of the finished pot. When forming the clay you can use wet fingers and do it by hand, or else use a palm sized stone or smooth piece of gourd or wood to spread the clay evenly.

When the clay has set for a short time, fifteen or twenty minutes, it can be removed from the form and given final shaping. Once the base is shaped it must be smoothed all over with moistened fingers or a piece of moistened leather or gourd and lightly rubbed on the surfaces. The edges need to be kept even and smooth. Turning the base upside down and pressing it slightly against a non-sticky surface will make the process of evening the edge easier.

A cloth ring can be used to support the smoothed base; or a saucer, into which the base can be turned when being removed from the form. For larger pieces, native potters learned by experience that sand makes a good support for the base. It is best, when using sand, to place a piece of cloth—cheese-cloth, canvas, or even plastic baggies—between the base and the earth. The base cannot be built upon yet, but should be allowed to set in place until it becomes leather hard. Clay is leather hard when the surface is tacky but not wet, and holds its shape under slight pressure while still being workable.

Using fingers, or paddle and stone anvil, the upper part of the base can now be worked into proper size and shape. To use the paddle and anvil you place the stone anvil on the inside of the pot and lightly slap the outside with the paddle. The base must be 5/8″ to 3/4″ thick at the bottom, 1/2″ to 5/8″ thick at the upper edge. The base, fingers, paddle and stone anvil must all be kept moist for this part of the process.

Next the edge must be prepared to accept and hold the coils. This is done by taking a sharp stick—a toothpick will do fine—and "scoring" the edge; making small, shallow marks in the clay to roughen it, creating more surfaces whereby to connect to the coil placed upon it. In fact, this process of roughing joined surfaces is required any time two pieces of clay come together. If left smooth the coils will separate, not holding to the base or each other as the walls are built.

The walls are shaped with the fingers and a piece of gourd, which is the same shape as the interior, or a paddle and stone anvil. Pieces of wood, gourd, bone, and stone used to shape and smooth pots, in a variety of shapes and sizes, were highly prized, and handed down from one generation to the next.

Some of Doris' burnishing stones were analyzed and

Rolling the first coil, or "snake," of clay to be
attached to the base. Note cloth ring next to the
bowl, which will be used to support the base as coils
are applied; this helps the base retain its shape as
pressure is applied when coils are added.

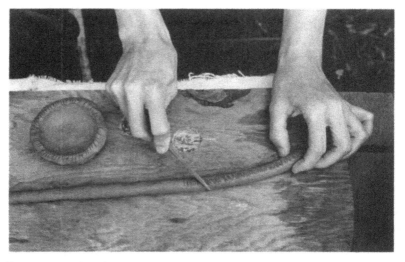

Incising the base and the coil to insure they bond
completely. The coil is scored on both sides in
preparation for the next coil. Incisions are criss-
crossed.

found to be such marvelous objects as mastodon tusk and saber tooth tiger teeth! Some of my personal favorites were gathered at the base of Alaskan glaciers, from the shores of Arctic rivers, and from the alpine cliffs of the Rockies. It often takes a long time to find a stone the right size and shape to be useful on many types of pots.

When the edge is roughened up and moistened, take a handful of clay to make the first coil. Roll the hunk of clay, or ball if already prepared, between your palms to form a "snake" of clay long enough to go around the edge of the base one-and-one-half to three times. Clay coils over a foot long are hard to handle. Shorter coils take longer to work into a pot, but are easier to work with. How long a coil you use must be judged in relation to your experience and confidence. The coil needs to be between 1/2" and 1" in diameter for most small and medium sized pots.

Remember to also roughen the contact surfaces where coils meet to help the clay adhere and form a good seal. A sharp forked instrument works well for scratching the surfaces.

Hold the coil in one hand, a few inches above the top edge of the base, and with the other hand guide the end of the coil into place. Put your fingers on the interior and use them to press the coil downward and outward, and use your thumb to press the outside of the coil downward and inward.

Secure the coil firmly to the rim but don't use too much pressure, for this will cause the base to crack or lose its shape. Should this happen, stop with the coil, and repair or rebuild the base. Making several bases to begin with will make this eventuality easy to resolve. Then, pressing lightly, repeat the process until you can get the coil once around the base. Repeat the process until the coil ends.

It will take from one to three coils to make the body of most pots. Larger pots will require thicker coils. It is possible to make exquisite, even thin-walled pottery, with very thin

Note how the coil is shaped as it is applied; and that the base has been set in the cloth ring.

First coil applied to both bases. The smaller base doesn't need a supporting ring because it is small enough to be supported in the palm of the hand.

coils, but it takes some experience first. Begin small and simple.

A short time is allowed to pass between the addition of coils to allow the freshly attached coil to set—ten to fifteen minutes at most, and less in a hot, dry climate where you may even have to speed up your work to keep pace with fast drying. Don't forget to moisten the scored contact surfaces as you apply the coil.

After adding two or three coils, use your fingers, a piece of gourd, a stone, or the paddle and anvil to smooth the coils and to shape and even them out. Thinner pots might require shaping and smoothing more often. As a general rule the coiled walls of the clay "body" will form at least 2/3 of the pot, depending on its shape.

If you add a neck to the pot it is usually 1/2 the circumference of the pot or less, and is usually no larger than the base at its widest point. The neck is made in the same basic manner as the body of the pot, though a longer, slimmer paddle, and a thinner stone, or even just a finger and thumb are used for shaping.

When the pot is finished, or when the neck is done if you build one, it is again allowed to harden for ten or fifteen minutes. Then you add the rim coil, which tops off and evens out the completed pot, using the same method as was used to apply the first coil to the edge of the base. The rim is made entirely by hand, and no two rims are alike, even when the bodies are molded. Each pot is unique, and will be made of different numbers, thicknesses, and lengths of coils.

The completed pot is allowed to set. Then, if you desire, you can incise, impress, or paddle on designs. Often a cord, or vine was wrapped around the paddle and used for decorating. Different surfaces and types of wood create different designs. If no decoration is desired at this point, the pot can be smoothed with leather—in modern pottery a small natural sponge is sometimes used for the same purpose—and allowed

Shaping the lip of the pot to an even, rounded thickness with the anvil/burnishing stone.

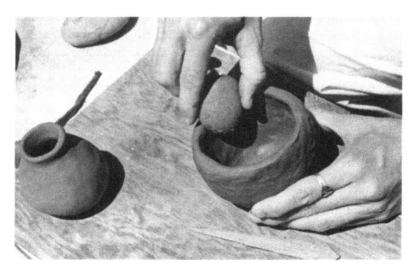

Completed coil pots. The ones on the upper left and right have been shaped and smoothed, and the lower one is being shaped. With a pot such as the one on the upper right, shaping and smoothing are done as you go along.

Burnishing the bottom of a pot by rubbing it with a stone.

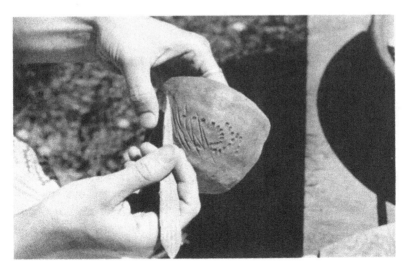

Incising designs with a sharpened stick on the outside of a completed coil pot.

to dry completely. Details on designs and decorations follow later.

Occasionally the coils are not smoothed, and are left to dry intact. Some of the People of this continent even bypassed the use of a base, and began the pot with a coiled bottom. But it is best to completely smooth both the inside and outside of pots at first. This is both a way of strengthening the pot, and of getting practice.

When the pot is dried it is ready for sanding and decoration. After that it will be ready for firing, which brings out the true natural brilliance of both the artist's decorations and the minerals in the clay.

Among many North American tribal cultures pottery is

The author painting the outside of a completed, smoothed coil pot with "slip," a thin slurry of clay and water, which, when almost dry, is then burnished with a polishing stone to a shiny smoothness.

made only by the women, though there are tribes where men take on various parts, such as the firing or the decorative work. Mostly though, the methods and materials were handed down from mother to daughter.

Molds and Hollowed Forms

A mold is a two-sided negative copy of an object which may have ceased to exist. Using a mold is the opposite of using a form. Clay is placed over a form, and into a mold. Molds are traditionally made in various ways, depending on the tribe; such as carved from wood or stone, made of fired clay, or made of other localized materials such as baskets, or large bones.

Use of molds was a later development among many tribes, and often the result of settled, communal life. Such molds were used to preserve traditional and ceremonial forms of pottery. Molds also make the potting process faster and easier. When people began to trade extensively, and popular designs became widespread, speed of production was a valuable innovation.

To mold clay, you must first make or obtain a mold. Modern potters use plaster of paris to make molds. Next you simply coat the inside to prevent sticking, impress clay into both halves, leaving some excess, and then press the two halves of the mold together. The clay is allowed to set and dry a while, during which time it will shrink some.

When the clay has partially dried, the object is removed from the mold. The outside contours are shaped and smoothed, and the hollow portion carved out. Most molded pieces were small, although some larger ones must surely have existed which have been lost to time.

Such objects as pipe bowls, figurines and totems, small effigy bowls and objects, and other likewise small pieces are best made using molds. Cups, small bowls, water jars, and food storage containers—many daily useful objects similar to those found in today's kitchens—were also often made in this way.

The mold must, of course, be bound together with twine, rope, or rubber bands while the pot sets. Compressing the clay together forms a strong bond.

The hollowing out process is accomplished using a stick, spoon, or wire loop, depending on the size and delicacy required. Dig out as much clay as is necessary, making the opening and hollow area large enough to be smoothed out with moist fingers, or, if large enough, a smooth stone.

Beautiful, functional, and strong pottery is produced using this technique. Another method for making hollow pots was to make the two halves by hand and then join them together. Only some tribes used this method. It is useful for making small pots, animal forms, and pieces with designs carved through the walls. Such pots are usually more decorative than functional, which attests to the more modern nature of the technique.

Some molds, just like shaping and burnishing stones, have been handed down from the grandmothers for countless generations. And even though men did not traditionally make pottery, in our time and place anyone can do it, using methods as old and varied as the People who have always lived in this land.

Beads, trinkets, commemorative pieces, trade items, and jewelry of clay are among the many things these People made, and continue to make to this day.

Over time, as with most crafts and arts, a certain limited selection of forms and varieties of pottery came into existence which were common to all tribes, but which show unending diversity from person to person and tribe to tribe.

It must be noted that the people native to the American continent accomplished feats of craft and prehistoric engineering without a written language or any form of mathematics as we know it. Problems were solved by intuition and experience.

Decorating, Slipping, and Burnishing

At this point you should have a completed, rough-surface pot that is almost dry, but still moist enough to incise designs, or create decoration using relief carving.

You can impress designs with a strong, thin, sharply pointed stick—or a toothpick—or use larger, rounded objects, such as stone, wooden marking tools, or objects like rope, leaves, and whatever else your imagination comes up with to impress into the clay.

Incising a design is done by actually rubbing or cutting away clay with a knife or sharp stone in a regular pattern, and can be taken a step further when used to create an image or design in relief. Many beautiful examples of such pottery decoration, applied to a yet moist pot, are still to be found, both in museums and coming from the fires of those who carry on this traditional craft.

Another way to cover a still moist surface with a regular, but more varied pattern is to take a paddle, like the one used with the stone anvil, and wrap it with twine or string. In a traditional setting, cord made of plant fiber was often used. Then pat the design onto the pot with strokes just heavy enough to make the kind of markings you want. This same technique can be used with slip, and works best with moister pots. If the pot is too dry, or you pat too hard, damage could result.

To incise a wide pattern into the moist pot, let it dry, and paint it with slip of contrasting color. You can then use a razor to carve through it to the contrasting color of the pot. This is called "sgraffito," covered later.

To apply slip—which is a slurry or mud, about the thickness of good enamel paint, skimmed from the top of clay buckets or mixed up from powder and water—you must first sand the pot. Use a medium rough sandpaper (80-120) to smooth and perfect the shape of the clay body.

If you choose not to further decorate the pottery, after incising a design, next dry and prepare to fire it. But you can continue, and use methods of decorating pottery that are very old. They may look and sound easy, but it takes quite a bit of practice to master the techniques before you create a decoration that looks like you want it to. Then it's possible to create very nice pieces using simple designs and methods.

The older methods were replaced by easier, faster ones over the centuries, methods the People hoped would both strengthen and further beautify the pottery they produced. As a result, fine work of great diversity and artistry was created, and is still being created today by modern Native craftspeople. Most pottery is a fusion of old and new; many designs are timeless.

Designs commonly used by North American natives were derived from their surroundings, myths, and everyday life. Some of the earliest and simplest decorative designs represent mountains, mesas, and rivers. Stylized human and animal forms were occasionally used, but natural forms such as the sun, moon, and stars, clouds, rocks, and life represented the world above and below. Other, more abstract designs emerged from myth and daily life, and the thoughts of native thinkers. The diversity, on a continental scale, is great, and yet each artist's work is unique.

Some designs came to mean more than one thing, or meant different things to differing tribes, so it is not always correct or appropriate to assume the meaning of a particular design. That depended on locale and point of origin. Should you wish to know the true meanings of ancient pictographs and designs, it is best to go to tribal elders or potters. And

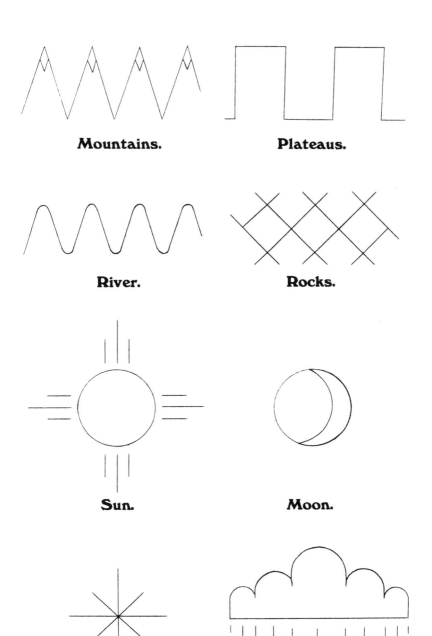

Mountains.　　　　**Plateaus.**

River.　　　　**Rocks.**

Sun.　　　　**Moon.**

Star.　　　　**Cloud.**

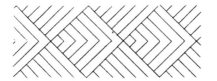

Friendship.

Stairway to Heaven.

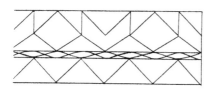

Journey.

Painted Plate.

often, what they give is ambiguous, or fanciful.

Such designs as those used by the Cherokee to represent friendship, spiritual progress (called "stairway to heaven"—where the pot is left with coils showing, upon which the design is incised), and journeys through new terrain, were all abstract representations that developed as a peoples' pottery did.

Floral designs, rain motifs, animal representation, feather shapes, and anything the eye can find, found their way onto pots. Effigies of animals or totems, pots that commemorated events, such as the wedding vase pictured with Doris Blue on page 10, pots that represented visions, spiritual beings, or personal relations were all fashioned by a common methodology used for thousands of years before potter's wheels and kilns came into being.

Catawba potters often burnish their pots without adding designs, prefering to let the fire color the piece. The Cherokee burnished sometimes, but are also well known for textured pots and fine designs. Most pottery of the Southwest is sanded, slipped, burnished, and painted.

Recently a friend gave me a piece of pottery found in the desert below the cliffs where the ancestors of the Pueblo, Navaho, and other desert tribes had dwelt at least a thousand years ago. This pottery is of finely textured grayish clay with undertones of purple tint from trace minerals and tiny mica chips. It is burnished on the outside and painted with a pattern in fine black lines that form an incomplete design.

What is amazing about this pottery fragment is that it is almost indistinguishable from fragments of pots made by myself and others who have learned the simple, yet timeless methods involved. The walls of this piece of pottery are about three-eighths of an inch thick, appearing to have come from near the top of the piece it originally belonged to. Techniques and rules have been consistent for thousands of years.

In another decorative method, called "sgraffito," slip is applied to the pot that is different in color than the clay of the pot. A design is incised through the moist slip to reveal the contrasting background color. A sharp blade is required to do this well. If slip is overly dry the edges of the design will not be sharp. This is all right, if you burnish the edges smooth, but inevitably the two colors of clay mix together.

Both the Cherokee and Navaho are famous for developing methods of making polished blackware, which is an extremely shiny, bluish-black pottery that is impregnated with carbon from the reduction medium used during the firing. The Cherokee used an earthen mound kiln to make this highly durable earthenware, and put in fine wood chips of cedar, pine, oak, and maple in layers. The Navaho used a smaller mound created by burning a dome of animal dung (horse or cow dung will do, although buffalo chips were in common usage before the arrival of domestic breeds of animals) over the pottery, which had been preheated and fired with wood. Larger wood pieces were used, causing the dome to collapse in a mound wherein temperatures would reach in excess of 1500 degrees.

The Catawba used sticks and bark to reduce their pots,

which created a multi-colored finish, much like the finish obtained by the Hopi when they used a large pile of dry grass for the same purpose. In each case the pots received oxygen during the reduction phase, while in the Cherokee and Navaho methods all oxygen was cut off.

We are now to the point of covering the specifics of applying various decorative designs and colors before firing.

Take the dried pot in hand, sand it relatively smooth with medium grit sandpaper (80-120 grit will do), and make sure to shape the pot evenly all over as you work. Don't make the top edge of the pot thinner than the walls of the top inch of the pot. If the lip gets too thin it cracks easily (take care when building pots to anticipate some loss during sanding).

Check for cracks that would prevent the pot from making the journey through the fire. If it is a coil pot, be certain that all the coils dried tightly joined, and that there are no hairline fractures at the joints.

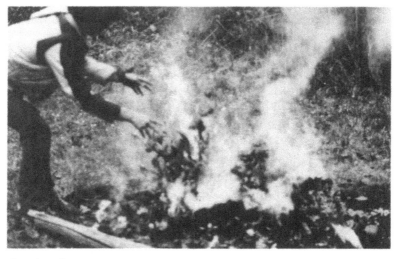

Author's assistant covering the firing pit with dry leaves to reduce the fire after the pots have been heated to the highest possible temperature.

Apply light, even pressure so as not to oversand. Once the pot is sanded it is ready for the application of slip. Slip is applied with a medium sized brush to the outside of the pot, except the center of the bottom, which can be left with the slightly rougher finish. Slip can also be applied to the upper part of the inside of the pot if desired.

Slip needs to be of even consistency and free of any rough particles. Generally speaking, it must be thin enough to spread evenly and well, but thick enough to cover without running or too much soaking in. If it's too thin it won't build up and will come off when burnished. Slip is best when about the consistency of modern house paint.

If the slip is just right, and applied correctly, it can be taken care of in one layer, but several layers can be applied, allowing several minutes between coats. Once the pot is slipped it is allowed to dry for a few hours before painting on a design, although you can often burnish the slip just a short while later, in fifteen or twenty minutes on a hot, dry day.

Usually slip is of the same, or nearly same, color of clay as the pot it covers, but it doesn't have to be, as in sgraffito. Regardless of color, slip needs to be of similar constitution to that of the pot, of the same clay if possible, as there could be cracking of the slip if it is too different a composition. This is because clays of different composition expand and contract at different rates during both drying and firing.

Once your pot is slipped and almost dried (it will begin to lighten up in color at this point) you will need to smooth the surface to a glass-like finish through the process of burnishing.

Using a very smooth stone of the appropriate shape and size to rub the nearly dried slip, you can create a striking finish that is glass-smooth. Rub the slipped parts of the pot very lightly back and forth, just enough to completely smooth the surface without marking it or going through it.

Once the pot is burnished it can be fired after drying, or

you can paint designs on the smooth surface with a fine brush and thin slip. The slip is set when it lightens up in color and no longer feels tacky to the touch.

The slip used in painting on designs is often the same as the slip used to cover the pot overall, but it is slightly thinner in consistency. Some tribes mix various mineral and vegetable agents with this slip to give it contrasting color.

You can paint traditional designs, garnered from books, museum pieces, and collections, invent designs, or use totally abstract paintings on your pots. Potters of the Southwest do subtle, highly intricate, very artistic paintings on their pots. Most tribes of North America painted some of their pottery, depending on their lifestyle and locale.

Today, traditional methods have given way to modern. Pots are often thrown on wheels, fired in a conventional kiln, and painted with designs that are true to tradition as far as the eye goes, but not truly made in the old way by using gathered clay, few if any tools, slip finishes and paints, and an open firing method. The unique character of pottery made in the old way is the result of the interaction of people, methods, and materials from which it is composed, and this unique character suffers under modern alteration, although works of great beauty are created.

Pottery fired in electric or gas kilns, made with electrical appliances, and painted with acrylic, tempera, or poster paints serve the main purpose of preserving traditional motifs and designs into modern times.

Fortunately, although some things are lost over time and distance, there are still practitioners of the old styles and methods of using materials gathered from nature. After some study and practice any person can learn to duplicate the old styles, traditions, and decorations used since prehistoric times among Native peoples.

Once the pot is painted it is ready to be burnished one last time. Stones are one natural material used for burnishing.

Whatever is used must be perfectly smooth, large enough to hold comfortably, and of an overall shape that fits many types of pottery. A roughly triangular piece with rounded edges and tips is good.

Doris told me, when she showed me her own burnishing pieces, that some were handed down from generation to generation, and certain shapes and types were highly prized and sought after. Her stones are of indeterminate origin and age.

But for our purposes, any glassy, easy to hold object will do. I have even used a spoon when nothing else could be found! You simply rub lightly on the surface of the clay, using horizontal or vertical strokes, or alternating with both. Burnishing in only one direction insures a consistent finish.

Pots that are completely dried after slipping can still be burnished, although you may need to dip your burnishing tool in water every few strokes to insure complete smoothness. Dip the tool, rub the wetted portion lightly until dry, blow away the dust and move on to the next spot.

A burnished pot is stronger than an unburnished one. The surface's molecules are aligned into a better configuration through rubbing. Plus the pressed, aligned molecules of clay reflect light with their smoothness instead of diffuse it. A beautiful glassy finish that will last as long as the pot is thus created.

Burnishing not only adds beauty and strength, but increases the value of the pot. It must be done slowly and gently so as to fill and smooth over minor irregularities on the surface of the pot.

A well slipped and burnished pot will emerge from the firing unflawed and made to last. On occasion, minute, hairline fractures will appear in the finish after firing, but if these are only surface markings and the pot rings true then there is no need for concern.

In modern times scientific ceramicists have found that

through proper combination of elements a primitive sort of glaze can be created. A glaze is a liquid finish much like glass. By adding salt and potash to slips, in the form of mineral and vegetable powders, Native potters created finishes that were quite hard and durable.

Other cultures around the world also discovered this process, and the type of glaze created was given the name "pulse" glaze in modern times. The silicon, aluminum, sodium, and calcium harden at slightly higher temperatures respectively, so a sort of step burning was produced that created a finish harder than common in pottery with iron as its main third or fourth element.

You can develop your own methods and variations of materials, designs, and finishes as you practice and improve your skills in the making of North American pottery.

Remember, indigenous peoples learned their crafts from childhood and worked countless hours to refine and perfect their techniques for improving their pottery survival. So, don't be dismayed by flaws and unsuccessful attempts at this stage. Like any other labor-intensive craft it takes lots of time, patience, and love to create strong, enduring works of art. I have been doing pottery in this way for seven years, and still lose pots during building or firing every time. That is one of the difficult and wonderful things about making pottery this way: You can't be certain, until the pots have cooled, what you've got.

So, it is time to get on to the firing stage. Once your pot has been sanded, slipped, decorated, and burnished you are finished with the process of building and decorating and can set it on a shelf to dry thoroughly until firing time arrives, which is usually not for two to four weeks later.

Over the course of a few weeks you can build many pots. Start small, and use only a few pieces at first, so that things will be easier to handle. A small batch of pots means a small fire, which is easier to manage. After experience, you will begin to make larger and more pieces for each firing.

Native potters fire anywhere from just a few pieces to upwards of fifty or sixty pieces at one time, depending on the level of experience of the potter, and those doing the firing, if it's not the potter. Ten pieces is a good amount for a first firing. When you have that many pieces dried and ready, the firing process begins.

Firing Pottery Without A Kiln

Begin with a calm, clear, not too dry day. You will need a site suitable for a large camp type fire. Be certain to obtain any necessary fire permits or permission to use a site not under your control.

Any open spot, sheltered on two or three sides, is best. The less wind the better. The less the air moves the hotter the fire will burn. A mild afternoon breeze can be useful if it is constant. Variable wind causes broad temperature fluctuations in the firing pit, and this can cause breakage or cracking.

Access to water is useful, but not required. If no stream or faucet exists nearby, just keep a couple of large buckets of water on hand.

Not following safety precautions and applicable laws governing fire can turn happy landowners into irate citizens. Protect yourself and the environment. Wear appropriate clothing, and use gloves when your hands must get close to the fire. Following a few simple rules will insure both safety and well fired pottery.

Tools needed include a shovel to dig the pit, a hatchet, a rake or pitchfork, gloves or hot pads, tongs or a long forked stick, and an optional cookie sheet.

Firings can be conducted under cover such as that afforded by picnic areas, barbecue pits, and large indoor fireplaces. Traditionally a special site was chosen, away from the main camp fires, while in modern times even wood and cook stoves have been used.

Doris said that after the advent of the iron stove for cooking and heating, one elder potter was drying her pots on the warming tray above the stove fire box, and accidently knocked one into the fire. She left it, and it fired just fine, albeit at a low temperature which produces pottery that isn't as hard and durable as that fired in a larger, outdoor pit.

Such a low fired pot wasn't useful for much, but it worked fine as a display work, and for selling to tourists who would just put it on a shelf and never use it.

When you've located a good firing site, dig a pit big enough in diameter to contain all your pots and still have several inches to a foot left over around the edges to use for placing wood.

The area must be free of debris, and if grassy, a plug of grass the size of your pit must be removed. Insert your shovel several inches under the grass and gently slice the roots. The grass will peel right back and can be easily replaced later, or used to build up the edges of the pit for a more permanent site.

Photo of the shallow pit with wood to be used in the pit-firing method.

For firing ten to twenty pots of small and medium size, a circular, shallow pit, six to twelve inches deep, and two to three feet across will suffice. The walls and edges must be built up several inches above the surface with dirt or rocks.

Next the pit needs to be lined with heat deflecting materials such as ashes and old coals, flat stones, cinders, or sand. I have even heard of using charcoal briquettes! It sounds like a good idea.

If you do use stones for the edges of the pit or for lining it, to prevent damage to the pots, which are very delicate when heated, make sure they are of a volcanic sort that won't crack or explode at high temperatures. Test stones in a regular camp fire or on top of a wood stove with a protective border.

Should there be a prevailing afternoon breeze, leave an opening a few inches wide in the rim of the pit facing into the direction of air movement. This opening can later be used to control the draft somewhat. If it is calm, this is not a necessary step.

It's best to dig and prepare your pit a few days before using it. This way the exposed earth can dry out and the rim become settled and stable. Line the pit at this time with moist clay or ashes—or even charcoal briquettes—to prevent dissipation of the heat. The hotter the fire the harder the pottery.

When the pit is done you are ready to finish preparations for the firing, which lasts from four to twelve hours. Among the North American tribes there were, and still are, many variations in methods and materials adapted to local conditions and needs.

Some of the People used rocks among the coals to support the pots; some more modern methods use tin cans or sheet metal, wire or iron grates.

The simplest method is best for beginning. Variations can be attempted later. Place your pots directly onto the pile of red-hot coals built up in one of the traditional ways, after pre-heating.

Pots are as good as the maker and the fire, and timeless methods of burning clay bodies have always been done pretty much the same way. The way you fire and oxidize pots determines the results. A fire is a fire, and insofar as building methods go, they are universal. The greater variations come with the woods and other types of fuel, and with the reduction medium used, which is covered later in more detail. For now, with the pit prepared and the pots waiting to be fired, gather the wood and other materials for the fire.

There are several methods used to fire pottery by North American natives. The method described above is essentially Catawba, used in the southeastern part of the country. The Cherokee used a mound of earth three to four feet high, with draft holes in the bottom of a base just as wide as the mound was high. They placed alternate layers of wood chips and pottery into the chamber which was dug into the center of the mound. Then they lit it from below. The pots were fired up to four days, and came out black and quite hard. For pottery that didn't need be so durable the Cherokee used a method adopted from the Catawba, which was almost identical to their pit-firing process, only they dug no pit. They just built their fire on bare, flat earth. This method is one of the earliest and most common, and was used all across the continent, especially by semi-nomadic peoples, who needed moderately hard pottery that was portable and easy to produce.

More settled peoples, such as those of the Southwest, developed their own unique firing methods, more suited to local situations and materials. They too built the fire on bare, flat earth, but added a dome of buffalo, horse, cow, or other grass eating animal dung over the pots to increase the heat and protect pots during firing.

The Cherokee sometimes built a similar structure, but made of bark instead of animal dung. Such methods were continually modified and perfected over the ages, eventually leading to the beehive-shaped oven used to bake both bread

Completed, fully dried pots, being preheated next to the coals of a hardwood fire. They are turned periodically during the two or three hours of preheating to insure even temperatures.

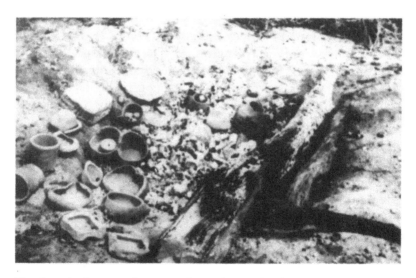

Preheated pots being placed on the hardwood coals to finish heating up to the same temperature as the coals.

and pottery all around the world in the early days of communal life.

Now sheet metal, tin cans, fifty gallon drums, and other modern containments have supplanted traditional ones such as stones, bark, earthen mounds, and animal droppings. Yet the People still impart their spirit into their earthenware art, rich in color, shape, texture, and tradition. It doesn't matter what methods and materials they use to express themselves; for they are unique cultures that once roamed freely across the wilds of North America.

⬖⬖⬖⬖⬖⬖

Now, back to getting your wood together.

You'll need enough wood for at least a four to six hour fire. The types of wood depend on the sort of firing you do. In this case we will do open pit firing, because it is the easiest and gives the best results, all things considered.

Get a mixture of soft and hard woods. If the mix leans a little more to the soft wood side, that's good. And should you live in an area where hard woods are difficult to find freely, you can use soft woods for the whole firing. This will require more attention to timing, but can work out just as well.

Hardwoods are from broadleaf, flowering trees. Of the numerous kinds, the most common and preferred hardwoods are oak, apple, walnut, cherry, maple, and alder. Every locality will vary in type and amount of available woods. Some areas of the country have little or no hardwood. If this is your situation check with local high school wood shops, lumber mills, furniture factories, construction sites, and other such work places where burnable scrap wood may be available.

Soft woods come from "evergreen," coniferous trees which usually, but not always, have needles instead of leaves. The most common, familiar soft woods are cedar, pine, fir, spruce, and redwood. All of these woods are excellent as they burn hot and evenly.

If you live in an area with abundant wood resources, there

should be no problem finding forest windfall, logging area residue, or beach driftwood, all useable when well seasoned and cut to appropriate length.

Pieces of wood about six or eight inches thick and one to three feet long are best. About one-fourth of a cord should be enough for even the largest firing, and for smaller, shorter firings, a campfire sized pile should do.

Ideally you need 40% hard wood and 60% soft woods for your firing. But, when it comes right down to it these days, if it can be burned for heat, it can probably be used to fire pots. You also need a small stack of kindling, and for later use as a reducing medium, a pile of sawdust or wood chips. Bark, grass, and dung can be used for more advanced, later firings, and must likewise be on hand when the fire is lit.

Paper, dry grass, or cardboard can be used to start the fire. If you use scrap paper or lumber, be sure it is clean, free of tars, nails, and paints. Use the kindling to get the hardwoods burning. Continue burning hardwood until you build up a pile of coals deep enough to almost fill the pit. Once you have this bed of glowing embers prepared, it is ready for the pots.

Hardwoods burn long and slow, and cooler than softer woods. Even, enduring heat is the key element here. It will take from two to four hours for the coals to build up to a constant heat and even depth. While building this fire up you should, at the same time, be preheating the pottery to the temperature of the pile of coals (about 500-800°F).

Traditionally, the dry pots were placed around the fire pit as the fire was being lit, then they were moved and turned gradually closer as the fire heated up, until they changed color. When the pots lightened up it was a sign they were about ready to be placed carefully on the coals.

These days Doris and other Native American potters use their kitchen ovens to preheat. The pots are placed in a cold oven on a cookie sheet. The oven is turned to 200°F., and the temperature is increased 50–100° every half hour, until the oven reaches 500–600°, at which point the pots are ready to be taken to the firing pit. It will take two to four hours to completely preheat your pots, in either case.

In slower burning firing, such as the mound and dung methods, the pots are placed in the middle of the enclosure before the fire is lit, and they preheat inside. But that way is more difficult for beginners and should be forgone. Learning to do a small, moderately fast firing will prepare you for more difficult methods.

If pots are preheated unevenly they can crack or explode either during pre-heating, or when they are introduced to the fire. So great care and attention must be taken during this part of the process. Usually, a uniform brownish-red color creeps over the pots when they are ready to fire. Also, be sure the pre-heated pots and the coals are close in temperature, which means you must avoid a flaming pile of coals in preference for the intensely glowing variety.

Take your time preheating, do it slowly, and in tune with the build-up of the fire in the pit. When the pots are ready, they can either be placed directly on the coals, if they are pre-heated near the firing pit, or they can be placed on a slab of wood an inch or two thick for carrying to the fire. In this way you can place the slab of wood with the pots on it directly onto the coals as a perishable support.

Smaller pieces will be ready first, so place them during preheating in a way that makes it possible to move them onto the coals first. Put small pieces in the middle, the hottest part of the fire, because they can usually endure the most stress.

Use tongs to avoid burns. Traditionally, a long, forked stick was used to place the pots, mouth down, onto the coals. Protect your hands. This sort of fire can singe the hair right off of your hands and forearms, so be careful.

Keep pots separated from one another, and don't bump them into one another when placing on the fire. Pottery cracks readily at this point. If pots won't sit upside down then set

them where they are most stable. Pots that won't sit upside-
down need to be filled with hot coals. A garden trowel is useful
for this task, or a broad, flat piece of wood. Beads, figurines,
and other small pieces can all sit together in the heart of the
fire.

The preheating is done when the pots are arranged on the
coals. You are ready to begin the firing stage. It is important to
not let pots remain unheated for more than a minute or two. If
the pottery cools too much it is likely to break. Be gentle, but
work as fast as you can.

Now to cover the pottery and increase the temperature of
the fire to its maximum, which is upwards of 1500°F. Use
small sticks and large chips of wood to surround and cover the
pottery to a depth of one to three inches.

If you still have unburned pieces of hardwood, pile them
up around the edges of the pit to use as a base for the soft
woods.

Next cover the entire pile of coals, and the pottery, with
larger pieces of wood. Use soft woods to build a "teepee," "log
cabin," or other sort of roughly shaped enclosure around the
coals and pottery. You can also use shingles, or slabs of wood
to build up a dome. In any case you must now entirely
surround the pots with fire. Make your pile of wood two or
three layers thick, and keep covering until the pots can no
longer be seen.

You have to move fast at this point to get the enclosure
built before it can catch fire and burn. At the same time avoid
placing much weight on the pottery while building enclosure
walls that will not forcibly collapse and damage it. When the
pots are completely surrounded their temperature equalizes
with that of the fire and the blaze begins to get quite intense.

This wooden firing chamber, actually a primitive kiln, is
the primary structure of this method. It is an intermediate step
between random placement of branches over the pottery
(Catawba), and the development of the domed dung, and then

mud ovens (still in use among the Southwestern tribes). The early development of this proto-kiln was the beginning of modern ceramics.

Essentially, the more enclosed the pottery is, the more heat will be held in to harden it. In modern, completely enclosed brick kilns, which are fired using gas or electricity, pots are burned for days at temperatures as high as 3000°F. This creates vitrified, impervious pottery that is more like glass than clay.

The firing chamber we have built will burn and be rebuilt as many as three or four times over a four hour period to completely fire the pottery to its maximum hardness. After one or two hours the pots will all have turned a uniform bright reddish-orange. After three to four hours they may even turn cherry red, at which point they are as hot as this method of firing allows them to become. Pots must remain reddish-orange to cherry red for at least two hours or more to reach maximum hardness.

Wood is the oldest fuel used to fire pottery, but others were found over time as needed. Once the perishable firing chamber evolved, efficiency was improved and further developments could then take place. Yet, no other method of firing will give forth the same results as an open pit, wood firing.

Later ovens were built by the People of North America out of mud, stone, or even metal. In modern times fire bricks are the most common material used to build kilns. The reuseable oven was an important development, and is still in use in many parts of the world, allowing further improved methods to be invented.

As the People became more settled and agriculturally oriented they depended more and more on their potters. Without clay vessels in which to store semi-perishable food items, some things would be scarce at times and create hardships for all. So improving methods was more than important, it was a matter of survival.

The wooden firing chamber has its advantages and disadvantages, just as do all forms of firing. But in one respect it will always remain unique: The coloration of the pottery is the direct result of the firing method. And in the method we are using here, the flames act as an unpredictable paint brush, bestowing colors and patterns on the pottery that cannot be anticipated.

After three to fours hours of hot, softwood firing, the wood can be allowed to burn down. When the pots just begin to visibly emerge from the smoke and ashes, it's time for the last step in the firing process, that of reduction.

The first step of the firing oxidizes the pottery and turns it a uniform reddish or brownish color, depending on the type of clay used. The reduction phase reduces the amount of oxygen near the pots. As a result the rapidly reduced atmosphere will become impregnated with carbon, which will then become impressed in the surface of the pots in a way that depends on too many factors to control.

If the reduction is total, as with dung, sawdust, and some metal enclosures, the pottery will come out a shiny bluish-black. If the reduction is partial, as most are, a variety of other colors—red, brown, beige, pink, and grey—will emerge from the surface of the pottery as it bakes in the fluctuating flames. This makes each pot singular, unique, and beautiful.

Trace elements in the clay, such as sodium, calcium, iron, and manganese will change colors (often to the opposite of their oxidized color) when reduced by the oxgen removal. Temperatures also vary haphazardly across the surface of the pottery, changing quickly and altering colors.

To reduce pottery cover the entire pit with sawdust, wood chips, dry grass, leaves, or bark to a depth of several inches at least, and up to more than a foot for extremely hot fires. Make certain your reducing medium is free of dirt, rocks, sand, or other impurities as they can ruin the smooth surface of an otherwise perfect pot.

Enough reduction medium must be used to smother the fire without putting it out. It must smolder for one half to one and a half hours—long enough to burn off the reduction medium and leave the pottery partially exposed in a bed of fine gray ash. You may have to add or remove some reduction medium in order to get it just right. Some practice is required to gain a little control over this part of the firing. Once you do achieve control you will have more say in how the pots are colored through placement and oxygen control.

Reduce the fire gradually, letting the burning brush of nature do its painting on the pots in a way that is older than human memory. Now stand back and relax. The firing process is almost done, but it will take several hours for the fire to die and the pots to become cool enough to remove from the ashes.

In good weather just leave the pots in the pit until twilight, when the world cools. If you don't finish the firing until dark, leave the pots in the pit overnight, and remove them at dawn the next day.

If you must remove the pots sooner, due to bad weather or just plain excitement, wait until you can pick a pot up with your bare hands and not get burned. The still quite warm pots can be set on the rim of the pit to cool for an hour or two, or until the heat dissipates. It is best, and recommended, to leave the pottery in the pit until it is cooled all the way. Otherwise you might remove them early, and cause minute flaws in a pot that might have been perfect.

After the pots are cooled, you remove them from the pit for cleaning. Traditionally this was done with feather fans and then a piece of doeskin or other soft leather. For our pottery a soft cloth will do as well. You will only need to dust the pottery at first. Later, any dust left can be wiped off with a barely moistened cloth, which will deepen the colors that emerge.

After the pots are removed from the pit, spread the ashes

to be certain the fire is out. Then, after the cool pots are dusted and cleaned, stand back at a distance and appreciate the wonder and mystery of nature, and its truths, which come through in the form and colors of the finished work.

After cleaning, a pot can be tested for trueness by tapping it lightly with your fingernail. It should "ring" with a sound of wholeness. If it is flawed it will "clunk" when tapped. Most potters destroy flawed pieces, but some have flaws so minor they can still be used for display.

If the pot rings true it is a finished piece of low-fire bisqueware, and is now ready for use, display, or sale. This sort of pottery makes excellent gifts, and can be seen in galleries across the country, both on and off Indian lands.

Such pottery is not impervious to water unless specially treated at either of two stages during the firing. One way is to use a piece of pitch pine as the support for your pottery when placed in the fire. By placing the pieces mouth downward on the slab of wood you make the soot and the dark, resinous smoke impregnate the inner surfaces of the pots, which gives a water resistant quality to them.

A second method is to take the pot from the fire with a forked stick as soon as the reduction phase is completed. You roll the pot out next to the pit and then fill it with ground corn cobs or wheat germ. The oils in these materials will give the walls a waterproof coating when you turn the pot back upside down in the dirt next to the firing pit and seal it to create a vacuum. The pot is allowed to cool in this position. Both methods are for the experienced, as they take much trial and error to do correctly. These methods don't work completely or perfectly every time, but are mentioned here for your information. Don't chance cracking a pot this way unless it *must* be waterproofed.

This type of pottery cannot be used for cooking. Native peoples would heat stones in the fire, clean them off when hot by pouring a little water over them, then put them in a clay cooking pot full of water to heat it.

One last note related to firing. If you want to fire pots in this way but are unable to do so because of bad weather or lack of a site, you can accomplish the same ends, on a limited scale, by using a good wood stove. The temperatures are somewhat lower, the pottery must be generally smaller in size, and the pots won't always be as durable, but they will still come out beautiful and useable.

Among some tribes animal fat was often used to polish and preserve pottery; applied by hand and rubbed in with soft leather. This gave the pots a fine protective lustre. Some of the People left the pottery as it came from the fire, as pots that are frequently used will absorb a lot of oil from hands, and over time will take on a soft glow as well.

Nothing quite equals the multi-colored, smoothly burnished finish of pots fired in this ancient way. Occasional dusting with a soft cloth is all that is required for display pieces, and those you sell or give as gifts.

If you wish to keep a pot that is cracked or broken (either from firing, mishandling, or old age) to display or use as a mold, you can usually glue it back together with almost any household glue and a lot of care. If you try this you will feel, firsthand, the experience of what museums must do to restore artifacts.

Pottery made in this time-honored method can be practical and useful, as it was for Native North Americans, or ornamental and decorative. Yet, in whatever way you use or look at it, the making of Native American pottery will reveal to you the fine collaboration existing between Mother Earth and the People of Clay.

Firing pit prepared by lining with stones first, then with ashes.

Preheated pots placed in hot coals on a slab of softwood. These pots were preheated in an oven to 500 degrees over a 2 to 3 hour period, then rushed from oven to coals on the slab.

Pots covered with thin slabs of wood; this is done very carefully so as to avoid damaging the pots, and to establish a base upon which more wood will be placed.

Domed wooden firing chamber completed. Other types of materials are used by various tribes. Dome must be rebuilt several times as it burns off.

Appendix A

List of Materials

Finding and processing native clay:
Shovel
Bucket
Hammer
Screen (large mesh)

Working Clay:
Solid table
Large knife
Wire with handles (for cutting clay)

Hand Building:
Clay, both workable and as dry powder
Water
Table/Lap board
Burnishing stones (or bones) of various sizes and shapes
Stick, paddle, sharp stones—for applying designs
Rag ring or a saucer: to sit pots in while shaping them
Piece of gourd or leather
Old wooden or clay bowl or plate (for use as a mold)
Sandpaper
Slip (fine slurry of clay used to paint designs onto pots)
Small brush

Firing:
Site
Paper to start the fire
Shovel, bucket of water
Rake or pitchfork (ax/hatchet optional)
Wood: kindling, hardwood, softwood (oxidation)
(briquettes)

Bricks or stones (50 gal. drum, or dirt mound) (concrete
blocks)
Grate, or sheet metal optional
Bark, wood chips, sawdust, dung, dry grass, or dry leaves
(for reduction)
Good weather for a fire (or a good wood stove)
Bran, grated corn cobs, or pitch pine chips
(for waterproofing)
Long, hooked or forked stick, or a pair of tongs
Gloves (optional)
Cookie sheets (optional, or slab of softwood)

Finishing:

Soft cloth or piece of leather (brush optional)
Lard or olive oil (optional)
Household glue for repairs

Last dome beginning to burn off.

Dome burned off and pots covered with coals and ashes.

Reduction medium burning off. Wooden slabs placed around the edges of the pit to help contain heat to the end of the firing.

Fired pots amid dust and cinders next morning, after cooling all night.

CPSIA information can be obtained
at www.ICGtesting.com
Printed in the USA
FSHW021428291118
53914FS